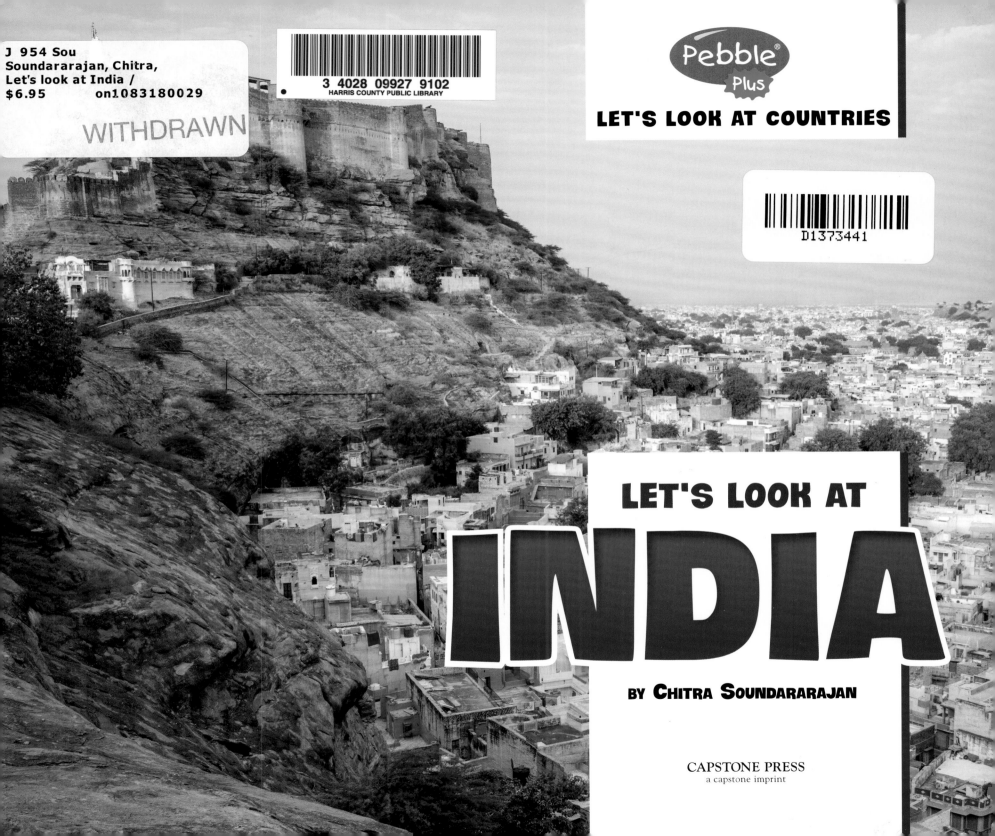

Pebble Plus

LET'S LOOK AT COUNTRIES

LET'S LOOK AT
INDIA

BY CHITRA SOUNDARARAJAN

CAPSTONE PRESS
a capstone imprint

Pebble Plus is published by Capstone Press,
1710 Roe Crest Drive, North Mankato, Minnesota 56003
www.mycapstone.com

Library of Congress Cataloging-in-Publication Data
Names: Soundararajan, Chitra, author.
Title: Let's look at India / by Chitra Soundararajan.
Description: First edition. | North Mankato, Minnesota: Pebble, a Capstone imprint, [2020] |
Series: Pebble plus. Let's look at countries | Audience: Grades K-3. | Audience: Ages 5-7.
Identifiers: LCCN 2019002063 | ISBN 9781543572100 (hardcover) | ISBN 9781543574746 (pbk.) |
ISBN 9781543572261 (ebook pdf)
Subjects: LCSH: India—Juvenile literature. Classification: LCC DS407 .S664 2019 | DDC 954—dc23
LC record available at https://lccn.loc.gov/2019002063

Editorial Credits
Jessica Server editor; Juliette Peters, designer; Jo Miller, media researcher; Laura Manthe,
production specialist

Photo Credits
Shutterstock: Ailisa, 17, Anna Jedynak, 18-19, D'July, Cover Middle, espies, 13, Globe Turner, 22
(Inset), ImagesofIndia, Cover Bottom, Cover Back, Lensalot, 8, nale, 4 (map), neha rathore, 4-5,
Ondrej Prosicky, 9, Rawpixel.com, 11, 16, Richie Chan, 1, Snehal Jeevan Pailkar, 15, Ultimate Travel
Photos, Cover Top, 6-7, Vivek BR, 2-3, 22-23, 24, YURI TARANIK, 20-21

All internet sites appearing in back matter were available and accurate when this book
was sent to press.

Note to Parents and Teachers

The Let's Look at Countries set supports national curriculum standards for social studies related
to people, places, and culture. This book describes and illustrates India. The images support early
readers in understanding the text. The repetition of words and phrases helps early readers learn
new words. This book also introduces early readers to subject-specific vocabulary words, which are
defined in the Glossary section. Early readers may need assistance to read some words and to use
the Table of Contents, Glossary, Read More, Internet Sites, Critical Thinking Questions, and Index
sections of the book.

Printed and bound in China.
1654

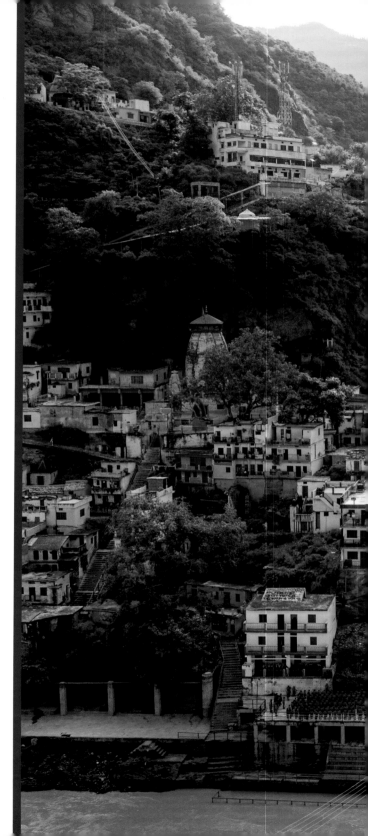

TABLE OF CONTENTS

Where Is India?

India is in South Asia. It is nearly one-third the size of the United States. Its capital is New Delhi.

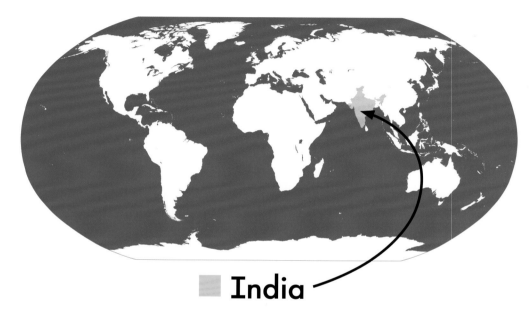

India

New Delhi

5

From Mountains to Deserts

The Himalaya Mountains are in northern India. The Thar Desert is in the west. South India's peninsula is surrounded by the Indian Ocean.

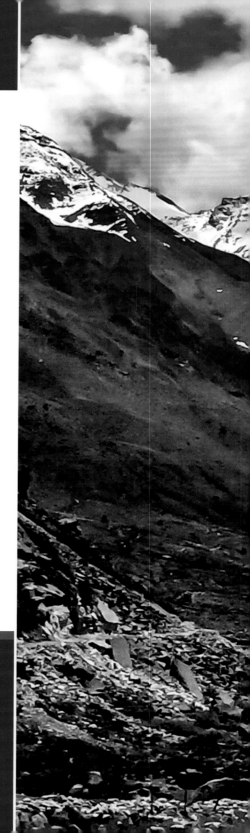

Himalaya Mountains

In the Wild

Exciting animals live in India. The Bengal tiger is the national animal. Herds of elephants roam the forests and parks. Kingfishers nest near rivers.

kingfisher

Bengal tiger

People

India is a diverse country. There are 22 different languages spoken in India. Hindi is the most common. Many people also speak English.

At the Table

Indian food changes by area.
Roti is eaten in the north. Roti is a round flatbread. People in the south eat more rice. Some Indian food, such as curries, can be spicy.

roti and curries

Festivals

Many festivals take place in India.

Families celebrate Diwali in the fall. It is the festival of lights.

Holi is the festival of colors. It marks the start of spring.

Diwali

On the Job

Many people in India work as farmers. They grow rice, wheat, and legumes. Some grow cotton. Many Indians make fabrics in factories.

Transportation

Most people in India travel by buses and trains. In cities streets are busy. People drive cars and ride motorbikes. Auto-rickshaws are also popular.

auto-rickshaws

Famous Site

The Taj Mahal is a monument in Agra. An emperor had it built in memory of his wife. It took more than ten years to build. Millions of people visit the Taj Mahal each year.

INDIA QUICK FACTS

India's flag

Name: Republic of India

Capital: New Delhi

Other major cities: Chennai, Mumbai, Kolkata

Population: 1,296,834,042 (July 2018 estimate)

Size: 1,269,219 square miles (3,287,262 sq km)

Language: 22 official languages (no national language); Hindi and English used in government

Money: Indian rupee

GLOSSARY

capital—the city in a country where the government is based

curry—a blend of spices that is used to flavor many foods; curry is also the name for a spicy, stew-like dish

diverse—different from one another

legumes—plants such as beans and peas

monument—a statue or building that is meant to remind people of an event or a person

peninsula—a piece of land with water on three sides

rickshaw—a small carriage that is usually pulled by a person; some rickshaws use a motor

READ MORE

Bajaj, Varsha. *T Is for Taj Mahal*. New York: AV2 by Weigl, 2016.

Joshi, Anjali. *Let's Celebrate Diwali*. Somerville, MA: Bharat Babies, 2017.

Perkins, Chloe. *Living in . . . India*. New York: Simon Spotlight, 2016.

INTERNET SITES

National Geographic Kids: India
https://kids.nationalgeographic.com/explore/countries/india

National Geographic Kids: Diwali
https://kids.nationalgeographic.com/explore/diwali

CRITICAL THINKING QUESTIONS

1. What animal in India would you most like to see? Why?

2. Indian food changes throughout the country. What food is common where you live?

3. Which of India's festivals would you most like to see? Why?

INDEX